A MESSAGE TO GARCIA
AND OTHER ESSAYS

A MESSAGE TO GARCIA

AND OTHER ESSAYS

BY

ELBERT HUBBARD

AUTHORIZED EDITION

NEW YORK
THOMAS Y. CROWELL COMPANY
PUBLISHERS

9—73
PRINTED IN THE
UNITED STATES OF AMERICA

PUBLISHER'S PREFACE

BY special arrangement with The Roycrofters we are privileged to republish these papers from the writings of "Fra Elbertus." In the author's "Apologia" he tells the circumstances of writing *A Message to Garcia*, a document which is destined for immortality. The two succeeding papers strike the same high note of responsibility and service.

Elbert Hubbard himself exemplified many of his teachings. He was strong, individual, self-made. Born in 1859, at Bloomington, Illinois, he had only a common-school education, but was an omnivorous reader. His experiment in founding The Roycroft Shop, at East Aurora, New York, devoted to the manufacture of de luxe books, simply carried out a lifetime ambition. Because of his somewhat radical theories and his broad-gauge handling of the labor problem, the experiment was watched elsewhere with much interest. He lived to see it an established success.

Mr. Hubbard toiled early and late.

While he was building the Roycroft Shop he founded and carried on two magazines, *The Philistine* and *The Fra,* and actually wrote a greater part of their contents. But that was not all. He wrote a series of 182 biographies under the general title of "Little Journeys to the Homes of the Great." This work was continued without a break for fourteen years!

Still fearing that he should rust out rather than wear out, he went on the lecture platform, and in his public speaking —thanks to his well-stored mind—he was as great a success as in his writing. His engagements were limited only by his physical endurance.

Few men have equalled him in energy or in output. He was a human dynamo. His production increased with the years, and was cut short by his untimely end, when the *Lusitania* was struck by a German torpedo and went down, May 7, 1915.

Says Franklin K. Lane: "He was a twentieth century Franklin in his application of good sense to modern life." And Thomas A. Edison adds: "He was of big service to me in telling me the things I knew, but which I did not know I knew, until he told me."

"A Message to Garcia" has had probably the most striking success of any short essay of recent times. This success came as a surprise to Mr. Hubbard no less than to others who at first did not realize its outstanding merits.

The man who carried the message, and was thus immortalized by Hubbard, was Colonel Andrew Summers Rowan, who at the outbreak of the Spanish-American War was a young lieutenant in the United States Army. When President McKinley asked of Colonel Arthur Wagner, head of the Bureau of Military Intelligence, "Where can I find a man who will carry a message to Garcia?" the reply was prompt.

"There is a young officer here in Washington named Rowan who will carry it for you," answered Colonel Wagner.

"Send him!" the President ordered tersely.

Lieutenant Rowan started within twenty-four hours, and with no other guard except native Cubans, who were furnished him by the patriots as soon as he secretly landed on the island. He penetrated the interior, and succeeded in reaching the revolutionary General. The story which he himself modestly related bristles with colorful incidents. Fortune undoubtedly favored him, but behind it all was the indomitable pluck of a young American who was determined to do his duty. General Miles, then commanding the United States Army, recommended a decoration for his subaltern, saying: "I regard the achievement as one of the most hazardous and heroic deeds in military warfare."

CONTENTS

APOLOGIA

THIS literary trifle, *A Message to Garcia,* was written one evening after supper, in a single hour. It was on the Twenty-second of February, Eighteen Hundred Ninety-nine, Washington's Birthday, and we were just going to press with the March *Philistine.* The thing leaped hot from my heart, written after a trying day, when I had been endeavoring to train some rather delinquent villagers to abjure the comatose state and get radioactive.

The immediate suggestion, though, came from a little argument over the teacups, when my boy Bert suggested that Rowan was the real hero of the Cuban War. Rowan had gone alone and done the thing —carried the message to Garcia.

It came to me like a flash! Yes, the boy is right, the hero is the man who does

his work — who carries the message to
Garcia.

I got up from the table, and wrote *A
Message to Garcia.* I thought so little of
it that we ran it in the Magazine without
a heading. The edition went out, and
soon orders began to come for extra copies
of the March *Philistine,* a dozen, fifty, a
hundred; and when the American News
Company ordered a thousand, I asked one
of my helpers which article it was that had
stirred up the cosmic dust. "It's the stuff
about Garcia," he said.

The next day a telegram came from
George H. Daniels, of the New York
Central Railroad, thus: "Give price on
one hundred thousand Rowan article in
pamphlet form—Empire State Express
advertisement on back—also how soon can
ship."

I replied giving price, and stated we
could supply the pamphlets in two years.
Our facilities were small and a hundred
thousand booklets looked like an awful
undertaking.

The result was that I gave Mr. Daniels permission to reprint the article in his own way. He issued it in booklet form in editions of half a million. Two or three of these half-million lots were sent out by Mr. Daniels, and in addition the article was reprinted in over two hundred magazines and newspapers. It has been translated into all written languages.

At the time Mr. Daniels was distributing the *Message to Garcia,* Prince Hilakoff, Director of Russian Railways, was in this country. He was the guest of the New York Central, and made a tour of the country under the personal direction of Mr. Daniels. The Prince saw the little book and was interested in it, more because Mr. Daniels was putting it out in such big numbers, probably, than otherwise.

In any event, when he got home he had the matter translated into Russian, and a copy of the booklet given to every railroad employee in Russia.

Other countries then took it up, and

from Russia it passed into Germany, France, Spain, Turkey, Hindustan and China. During the war between Russia and Japan, every Russian soldier who went to the front was given a copy of the *Message to Garcia*.

The Japanese, finding the booklets in possession of the Russian prisoners, concluded that it must be a good thing, and accordingly translated it into Japanese.

And on an order of the Mikado, a copy was given to every man in the employ of the Japanese Government, soldier or civilian.

Over forty million copies of *A Message to Garcia* have been printed. This is said to be a larger circulation than any other literary venture has ever attained during the lifetime of the author, in all history— thanks to a series of lucky accidents.

E. H.

East Aurora,
December 1, 1913.

A MESSAGE TO GARCIA

IN all this Cuban business there is one
man stands out on the horizon of my
memory like Mars at perihelion.

When war broke out between Spain and
the United States, it was very necessary
to communicate quickly with the leader of
the Insurgents. Garcia was somewhere
in the mountain fastnesses of Cuba—no
one knew where. No mail or telegraph
message could reach him. The President
must secure his co-operation, and quickly.

What to do!

Someone said to the President, "There
is a fellow by the name of Rowan will find
Garcia for you, if anybody can."

Rowan was sent for and given a letter
to be delivered to Garcia. How the "fellow by the name of Rowan" took the
letter, sealed it up in an oilskin pouch,
strapped it over his heart, in four days

landed by night off the coast of Cuba from an open boat, disappeared into the jungle, and in three weeks came out on the other side of the Island, having traversed a hostile country on foot, and delivered his letter to Garcia—are things I have no special desire now to tell in detail. The point that I wish to make is this: McKinley gave Rowan a letter to be delivered to Garcia; Rowan took the letter and did not ask, "Where is he at?"

By the Eternal! there is a man whose form should be cast in deathless bronze and the statue placed in every college of the land. It is not book-learning young men need, nor instruction about this and that, but a stiffening of the vertebræ which will cause them to be loyal to a trust, to act promptly, concentrate their energies: do the thing—"Carry a message to Garcia."

General Garcia is dead now, but there are other Garcias. No man who has endeavored to carry out an enterprise where many hands were needed, but has been well-nigh appalled at times by the imbecility of the average man—the inability or unwillingness to concentrate on a thing and do it.

Slipshod assistance, foolish inattention, dowdy indifference, and half-hearted work seem the rule; and no man succeeds, unless by hook or crook or threat he forces or bribes other men to assist him; or mayhap, God in His goodness performs a miracle, and sends him an Angel of Light for an assistant.

You, reader, put this matter to a test: You are sitting now in your office—six clerks are within call. Summon any one and make this request: "Please look in the encyclopedia and make a brief memorandum for me concerning the life of Correggio."

Will the clerk quietly say, "Yes, sir," and go do the task?

On your life he will not. He will look at you out of a fishy eye and ask one or more of the following questions:

Who was he?

Which encyclopedia?

Where is the encyclopedia?

Was I hired for that?

Don't you mean Bismarck?

What's the matter with Charlie doing it?

Is he dead?

Is there any hurry?

Sha'n't I bring you the book and let you look it up yourself?

What do you want to know for?

And I will lay you ten to one that after you have answered the questions, and explained how to find the information, and why you want it, the clerk will go off and get one of the other clerks to help him try to find Garcia—and then come back and tell you there is no such man. Of course I may lose my bet, but according to the Law of Average I will not.

Now, if you are wise, you will not bother to explain to your "assistant" that Correggio is indexed under the C's, not in the K's, but you will smile very sweetly and say, "Never mind," and go look it up yourself. And this incapacity for indeperdent action, this moral stupidity, this infirmity of the will, this unwillingness to cheerfully catch hold and lift—these are the things that put pure Socialism so far into the future. If men will not act for themselves, what will they do when the benefit of their effort is for all?

A first mate with knotted club seems necessary; and the dread of getting "the bounce" Saturday night holds many a worker to his place. Advertise for a stenographer, and nine out of ten who apply can neither spell nor punctuate—and do not think it necessary to.

Can such a one write a letter to Garcia?

"You see that bookkeeper," said the foreman to me in a large factory.

"Yes; what about him?"

"Well, he's a fine accountant, but if I'd send him up town on an errand, he might accomplish the errand all right, and on the other hand, might stop at four saloons on the way, and when he got to Main Street would forget what he had been sent for."

Can such a man be entrusted to carry a message to Garcia?

We have recently been hearing much maudlin sympathy expressed for the "downtrodden denizens of the sweatshop" and the "homeless wanderer searching for honest employment," and with it all often go many hard words for the men in power.

Nothing is said about the employer who grows old before his time in a vain attempt to get frowsy ne'er-do-wells to do intelligent work; and his long, patient striving after "help" that does nothing but loaf when his back is turned. In every store and factory there is a constant weeding-out process going on. The employer is constantly sending away "help" that have shown their incapacity to further the interests of the business, and others are being taken on. No matter how good times are, this sorting continues: only, if times are hard and work is scarce, the sorting is done finer—but out and forever out the incompetent and unworthy go. It is the survival of the fittest. Self-interest

prompts every employer to keep the best
— those who can carry a message to
Garcia.

I know one man of really brilliant parts
who has not the ability to manage a business of his own, and yet who is absolutely
worthless to anyone else, because he carries with him constantly the insane sus-
picion that his employer is oppressing,
or intending to oppress, him. He cannot
give orders, and he will not receive them.
Should a message be given him to take to
Garcia, his answer would probably be,
"Take it yourself!"

Tonight this man walks the streets look-
ing for work, the wind whistling through
his threadbare coat. No one who knows
him dare employ him, for he is a regular
firebrand of discontent. He is impervious
to reason, and the only thing that can
impress him is the toe of a thick-soled
Number Nine boot.

Of course, I know that one so morally
deformed is no less to be pitied than a
physical cripple; but in our pitying let us

drop a tear, too, for the men who are striving to carry on a great enterprise, whose working hours are not limited by the whistle, and whose hair is fast turning white through the struggle to hold in line dowdy indifference, slipshod imbecility, and the heartless ingratitude which, but for their enterprise, would be both hungry and homeless.

Have I put the matter too strongly? Possibly I have; but when all the world has gone a-slumming I wish to speak a word of sympathy for the man who succeeds—the man who, against great odds, has directed the efforts of others, and having succeeded, finds there's nothing in it: nothing but bare board and clothes. I have carried a dinner-pail and worked for day's wages, and I have also been an employer of labor, and I know there is something to be said on both sides. There is no excellence, per se, in poverty; rags are no recommendation; and all employers are not rapacious and high-handed, any more than all poor men are virtuous. My heart goes out to the man who does his work when the "boss" is away, as well as when he is at home. And the man who, when given a letter for Garcia, quietly takes the missive, without asking any idiotic questions, and with no lurking intention of chucking it into the nearest sewer, or of doing aught else but deliver it, never gets "laid off," nor has to go on a strike for higher wages. Civilization is one long, anxious search for just such individuals. Anything such a man asks shall be granted. He is wanted in every city, town and village—in every office, shop, store and factory. The world cries out for such; he is needed and needed badly—the man who can "Carry a Message to Garcia."

THE BOY FROM MISSOURI VALLEY

BY THE BOY SCOUTS

THE BOY FROM MISSOURI
VALLEY

WELL, it wasn't so very long ago—
only about twenty-three years.

I was foreman of a factory, and he lived
a thousand miles away, at Missouri Valley, Iowa. I was twenty-four, and he was
fourteen. His brother was traveling for
the Firm, and one day this brother showed
me a letter from the lad in Missouri Valley. The missive was so painstaking, so
exact, and revealed the soul of the child
so vividly, that I laughed aloud—a laugh
that died away to a sigh.

The boy was beating his wings against
the bars—the bars of Missouri Valley—he
wanted opportunity. And all he got was
unending toil, dead monotony, stupid
misunderstanding, and corn-bread and
molasses.

There wasn't love enough in Missouri Valley to go 'round—that was plain. The boy's mother had been of the Nancy Hanks type—worn, yellow and sad—and had given up the fight and been left to sleep her long sleep in a prairie grave on one of the many migrations. The father's ambition had got stuck in the mud, and under the tongue-lash of a strident, strenuous, gee-haw consort, he had run up the white flag.

The boy wanted to come East.

It was a dubious investment—a sort of financial plunge, a blind pool—to send for this buckwheat midget. The fare was thirty-three dollars and fifty cents.

The Proprietor, a cautious man, said that the boy wasn't worth the money. There were plenty of boys—the alleys swarmed with them.

So there the matter rested.

But the lad in Missouri Valley didn't let it rest long. He had been informed that we did not consider him worth thirty-three dollars and fifty cents, so he offered to split the difference. He would come for half—he could ride on half-fare—the Railroad Agent at Missouri Valley said that if he bought a half-fare ticket, got on a train, and explained to the conductor and everybody that he was 'leven, goin' on twelve, and stuck to it, it would be all right; and he would not expect any wages until he had paid us back. He had no money of his own, all he earned was taken from him by the kind folks with whom he lived, and would be until noon of the day he was twenty-one years old. Did we want to invest sixteen dollars and seventy-five cents in him?

We waxed reckless and sent the money —more than that, we sent a twenty-dollar bill. We plunged!

In just a week the investment arrived. He did not advise when he would come, or how. He came, we saw, he conquered. Why should he advise of his coming? He just reported, and his first words were the Duke's motto: "I am here."

He was unnecessarily freckled and curiously small. His legs had the Greek curve from much horseback riding, herding cattle on the prairies; his hair was the color of a Tamworth pig; his hands were red; his wrists bony and briar-scarred. He carried his shoes in his hands, so as not to wear out the sidewalk, or because they aggravated sundry stone-bruises—I don't know which.

"I am here!" said the lad, and he planked down on the desk three dollars and twenty-five cents. It was the change from the twenty-dollar bill. "Didn't you have to spend any money on the way here?" I asked.

"No, I had all I wanted to eat," he replied, and pointed to a basket that sat on the floor.

I called in the Proprietor, and we looked the lad over. We walked around him twice, gazed at each other, and adjourned to the hallway for consultation.

The boy was not big enough to do a man's work, and if we set him to work in the factory with the city boys, they would

surely pick on him and make life for him
very uncomfortable. He had a half-sad
and winsome look that had won from our
hard hearts something akin to pity. He
was so innocent, so full of faith, and we
saw at a glance that he had been over-
worked, underfed—at least misfed—and
underloved. He was different from other
boys—and in spite of the grime of travel,
and the freckles, he was pretty as a
ground-squirrel.

His faith made him whole: he won us.
But why had we brought him to the mis-
erable and dirty city—this grim place of
disillusionment! "He might index the letter-book?" I ventured. "That's it, yes, let
him index the letter-book." So I went
back and got the letter-book. But the
boy's head only come to the top of the
stand-up desk, and when he reached for
the letter-book on the desk he had to grope
for it. I gave him my high-stool, but this
was too low.

"I know what to do," he said. Through
the window that looked from the office to

the shipping-room, he had espied a pile of boxes. "I know what to do!"

In a minute he had placed two boxes end to end, nailed them together, clinched the nails, and carried his improvised high-stool into the office.

"I know what to do!"

And he usually did; and does yet.

We found him a boarding-place with a worthy widow whose children had all grown big and flown. Her house was empty, and so was her mother-heart: she was like that old woman in *Rab,* who was placed on the surgeon's table and given chloroform, and who held to her breast an imaginary child, and crooned a lullaby to a babe, dead thirty years before.

So the boy boarded with the widow and worked in the office.

He indexed the letter-book—he indexed everything. And then he filed everything —letters, bills, circulars. He stamped the letters going out, swept the office, and dusted things that had never been dusted before. He was orderly, alert, active, cheerful, and the Proprietor said to me one day, "I wonder how we ever got along without that boy from Missouri Valley!"

Six months had passed, and there came a day when one of the workmen intimated to the Proprietor that he better look out for that red-headed office-boy.

Of course, the Proprietor insisted on hearing the rest, and the man then explained that almost every night the boy came back to the office. He had seen him. The boy had a tin box and letter-books in it, and papers, and the Lord knows what not!

Watch him!

The Proprietor advised with me because I was astute—at least he thought I was, and I agreed with him.

He thought Jabesh was at the bottom of it.

Jabesh was our chief competitor. Jabesh had hired away two of our men, and we had gotten three of his. "Jabe," we called him in derision—Jabe had gotten

into the factory twice on pretense of see-
ing a man who wanted to join the Ep-
worth League or Something. We had
ordered him out, because we knew he was
trying to steal our "process." Jabe was
a rogue—that was sure.

Worse than that, Jabe was a Metho-
dist. The Proprietor was a Baptist, and
regarded all Methodists with a prenatal
aversion that swung between fear and con-
tempt. The mere thought of Jabe gave
us gooseflesh. Jabesh was the bugaboo
that haunted our dreams. Our chief
worry was that we would never be able
to save our Bank-Balance alive, for fear
o' Jabe.

"That tarnashun Jabe has hired our office-boy to give him a list of our customers—he is stealing our formulas, I know,"
said the Proprietor. "The cub's pretense
of wanting a key to the factory so he
could sweep out early was really that he
might get in late."

Next day we watched the office-boy.
He surely looked guilty — his freckles

stood out like sunspots, and he was more bow-legged than ever.

The workman who had given the clue, on being further interrogated, was sure he had seen Jabe go by the factory twice in one evening.

That settled it.

At eight o'clock that night we went down to the factory. It was a full mile, and in an "objectionable" part of the town.

There was a dim light in the office. We peered through the windows, and sure enough, there was the boy hard at work writing. There were several books before him, a tin box and some papers. We waited and watched him copy something into a letter-book.

We withdrew and consulted. To confront the culprit then and there seemed the proper thing. We unlocked the door and walked softly in.

The boy was startled by our approach, and still more by our manner. When the Proprietor demanded the letter that he had just written, he began to cry, and then we knew we had him.

The Proprietor took the letter and read it. It was to Jimmy Smith in Missouri Valley. It told all about how the writer was getting on, about the good woman he boarded with, and it told all about me and about the Proprietor. It pictured us as models of virtue, excellence and truth.

But we were not to be put off thus. We examined the letter-book, and alas! it was filled only with news-letters to sundry cousins and aunts. Then we dived to the bottom of the tin box, still in search of things contraband. All we found was a little old Bible, a diary, and some trinkets in the way of lace and a ribbon that had once been the property of the dead Nancy Hanks.

Then we found a Savings-Bank Book, and by the entries saw that the boy had deposited one dollar every Monday morning for eleven weeks. He had been with us for six months, and his pay was two dollars a week and board—we wondered what he had done with the rest!

We questioned the offender at length. The boy averred that he came to the office evenings only because he wanted to write letters and get his 'rithmetic lesson. He would not think of writing his personal letters on our time, and the only reason he wanted to write at the office instead of at home was so he could use the letter-press. He wanted to copy all of his letters—one should be businesslike in all things.

The Proprietor coughed and warned the boy never to let it happen again. We started for home, walking silently but very fast.

The stillness was broken only once, when the Proprietor said: "That consarned Jabe! If ever I find him around our factory, I'll tweak his nincompoop nose, that's what I will do."

Twenty-three years! That factory has grown to be the biggest of its kind in America. The red-haired boy from Missouri Valley is its manager. Emerson says, "Every great institution is the lengthened shadow of a single man."

The Savings-Bank Habit came naturally to that boy from Missouri Valley. In a year he was getting six dollars and board, and he deposited four dollars every Monday. In three years this had increased to ten, and some years after, when he became a partner, he had his limit in the Bank. The Savings-Bank Habit is not so bad as the Cab Habit—nor so costly to your thinkery and wallet as the Cigarette Habit.

I have been wage-earner, foreman and employer. I have had a thousand men on my payroll at a time, and I'll tell you this: The man with the Savings-Bank Habit is the one who never gets laid off: he's the one who can get along without you, but you can not get along without him. The Savings-Bank Habit means sound sleep, good digestion, cool judgment and manly independence. The most healthful thing I know of is a Savings-Bank Book—there are no microbes in it to steal away your peace of mind. It is a guarantee of good behavior.

The Missouri Valley boy gets twenty-five thousand a year, they say. It is none too much. Such masterly men are rare; Rockefeller says he has vacancies for eight now, with salaries no object, if they can do the work.

That business grew because the boy from Missouri Valley grew with it, and he grew because the business grew. Which is a free paraphrase from Macaulay, who said that Horace Walpole influenced his age because he was influenced by his age. Jabesh has gone on his Long Occasion, discouraged and whipped by an unappreciative world. Jabe never acquired the Savings-Bank Habit. If he had had the gumption to discover a red-haired boy from Missouri Valley, he might now be sporting an automobile on Delaware Avenue instead of being in Abraham's Bosom.

We shall all be in Abraham's Bosom day after tomorrow; and then I'll explain to Jabesh that no man ever succeeded in a masterly way, excepting as he got level-

HELP YOURSELF BY HELPING THE HOUSE

HELP YOURSELF BY HELPING
THE HOUSE

LITTLE hotels often feature their clerks, while small tailors proudly put forth their cutters. But a big business is built by many earnest men working together for a common end and aim. It is planned by one man, but is carried forward by many.

A steamship is manned by a crew, and no one particular sailor is necessary. You can replace any man in the engine-room of the *Mauretania,* and she will still cross the ocean in less than six days.

In an enterprise that amounts to anything, all transactions should be in the name of the firm, because the firm is more than any one person connected with it. Clerks or salesmen who have private letterheads, and ask customers to send letters to them personally, are on the wrong track.

To lose your identity in the business is

one of the penalties of working for a great institution. Don't protest—it is no new thing—all big concerns are confronted by the same situation—get in line! It is a necessity.

If you want to do business individually and in your own name, stay in the country or do business for yourself.

Peanut-stands are individualistic; when the peanut-man goes, the stand also croaks. Successful corporations are something else.

Of course, the excuse is that, if you send me the order direct, I, knowing you and your needs, can take much better care of your wants than that despised and intangible thing, "the house." Besides, sending it through the Circumlocution Office takes time.

There is something more to say. First, long experience has shown that "the saving of time" is exceedingly problematic. For while in some instances a rush order can be gotten off the same night by sending it to an individual, yet when your individual has gone fishing, is at the ball-game, or is sick, or else has given up his job and gone with the opposition house, there are great and vexatious delays, dire confusions and a great strain on vocabularies.

This thing of a salesman carrying his trade with him, and considering the customers of the house his personal property, is the thought of only 2 x 4 men. A house must have a certain fixed policy—a reputation for square dealing—otherwise it could not exist at all. It could not even give steady work and good pay to the men who think it would be only a hole in the ground without them.

In the main, the policy of the house is right. Don't acquire the habit of butting in with your stub-end of a will in opposition to the general policy of the house. To help yourself, get in line with your house, stand by it, take pride in it, respect it, uphold it, and regard its interests as yours. The men who do these things become the only ones who are really necessary. They are Top - Notchers, Hundred - Pointers.

The worst about the other plan is that it
ruins the man who undertakes it. For a
little while, to do a business of your own
in the shadow of the big one is beautiful
—presents come, personal letters, invita-
tions, favors, is Mr. Johnson in! By and
by Johnson gets chesty; he resents it when
other salesmen wait on his customers or
look after his mail. He begins to plot for
personal gain, and the first thing you
know he is a plain grafter, at loggerheads
with his colleagues, with the interests of
the house secondary to his own.

We must grow towards the house, and
with it, not away from it. Any policy
which lays an employee open to tempta-
tion, or tends to turn his head, causing
him to lose sight of his own best interests,
seizing at a small present betterment, and
losing the great advantage of a life's business, is bad. The open cash-drawer, valu-
able goods lying around not recorded or
inventoried, free-and-easy responsibility,
good-enough plans, and let-'er-go policies,
all tend to ruin men just as surely as do

cigarettes, booze, pasteboards and the races.

The man who thinks he owns "his trade," and threatens to walk out and take other employees and customers with him, is slated to have his dream come true. The manager gives in—the individualist then is sure he is right—the enlarged ego grows, and some day the house simply takes his word for it, and out he goes. The down-and-outer heads off his mail at the Post-Office, and for some weeks embarrasses customers, delays trade and more or less confuses system, but a month or two smooths things out, and he is forgotten absolutely. The steamship plows right along.

Our egotist gets a new job, only to do it all over again if he can. This kind of a man seldom learns. When he gets a job, he soon begins to correspond with rival firms for a better one, with intent to take his "good-will" along.

The blame should go back to the first firm where he was employed, that allowed him a private letterhead, and let him get filled with the fallacy that he was doing business on his own account, thus losing sight of the great truth that we win through co-operation and not through segregation or separation. The firm's interests are yours; if you think otherwise, you are already on the slide.

The only man who should be given full swing and unlimited power is the one who can neither resign nor run away when the crash comes, but who has to stick and face the deficit, and shoulder the disgrace of failure. All who feel free to hike whenever the weather gets thick would do well to get in line with the policy of the house.

The weak point in Marxian Socialism, is that it plans to divide benefits, but does not say who shall take care of deficits. It relieves everybody of the responsibility of failure and defeat. And just remember this: unless somebody assumes the responsibility of defeat, there will be no benefits to distribute. Also this: that the man who is big enough to be a Somebody is also willing to be a Nobody.